Table of Contents

Introduction

Why is it wrong to rape? What made the Holocaust bad? What makes charity righteous? Why is it good to tell your significant other you love them? Throughout the history of philosophy, contemplatives have desperately attempted to decipher what exactly makes an action moral or immoral; more possible answers have been offered than any regular person could hope to abide by. These moral theories primarily include virtue ethics, deontology, relativism, utilitarianism, and, what is perhaps the most widely subscribed idea in the modern world, Divine Command. Each of these ideas, though vastly complicated, do not survive detailed scrutiny. In fact, in certain situations, many of the theories listed above will urge the agent to act in ways that are patently evil. An unfailing theory that encompasses every moral agent and perfectly guides the actions thereof is needed. Here, I will describe the Universal Ethic: an ethical code that coincides with most popular moral intuitions and objectively results in the maximal goodness in the world.

What is Ethics?

Before laying out the Universal Ethic, it is necessary to describe the meaning of ethics. When one asks the meaning of something, like when one asks what the meaning of life is, they usually mean one of two things: a) what is the definition of the word, or b) what is the *purpose* of the concept mentioned. In terms of ethics, these two questions are quite simple to answer. The definition of ethics is a branch of study concerned with the nature of goodness and badness. It deals with how something can have the quality of being good or bad and why some things are good and others are not. The purpose of ethics, on the other hand, is perhaps a bit more complicated. It seems uncontroversial to say that the purpose of ethics is to determine a way to maximize the overall goodness in the world. What exactly "goodness" is and how one is supposed to maximize it are crucial questions that I will answer later in this piece.

Ethics, though, is not just the study of goodness and badness; it is also about how one should act in the world. When faced with a decision, the most moral choice is *always* the one that should be picked. Because of this, ethics is essentially the study of decision making; it points toward what choice is best in every situation. Whether or not one should donate money to a local charity is an obvious moral decision, and so is whether or not one should buy a new car. Every dilemma one encounters has moral value because they all affect the life of oneself and the lives of others, either directly or indirectly: when to get married, when to buy a new phone, how to fire an employee, or even what to do on a Saturday afternoon. The most sublime and apposite mystery of one's life is which decisions should be made, and ethics gives a total blueprint on how one should conduct themselves all the way until death. It is a silent judge that should mediate every voluntary movement in one's body.

Each category of philosophy claims to be the crown of the discipline. Metaphysicians may assert they are studying the true fundamentals of philosophy because concepts such as time, space, and matter appear to be foundational to reality. Phenomenologist may make the same assertion because a case can be made that consciousness and the experience of reality is more elementary than metaphysics. Epistemologists can declare that knowledge takes priority over everything else in philosophy because how can any other concept be discussed if it is not clear what knowledge is or if it is even possible to attain? However, questions such as why is there something instead of nothing, why does experience have a qualitative aspect, or what does it mean to know something may be so difficult to answer that humans are incapable of success. What is certain about your life is that you are alive now, so the best question to ask is how should you act in the world to make existence better for yourself and those around you.

How did Humans Acquire a Sense of Morality?

Before going further, it is necessary to explain how humans acquired a sense of right and wrong in the first place. There is a multitude of theories that attempt to solve this puzzle, but for the sake of simplicity, I will argue why the most commonly held solution is incorrect and why animals have obtained moral intuition through evolution.

The most widely held ethical view in the modern world is that of Divine Command: the belief that what is moral and what is not is dictated by God. Whether or not God in this case is the Islamic Allah, the eastern Mahadeva, or an Omni-God would change the discussion. However, because it is necessarily related to all the deities listed above, I will continue with the most common form of God among digital natives: the Uncaused Cause.

It is a prevalent belief among some theists that mankind without God as the source/grounding of morality would devolve into a morally forsaken mess; God is what keeps each individual from torturing and killing their next-door neighbor. What exactly is meant by this assertion can be difficult to deduce. If what is meant is that those who do not believe in God are morally corrupt then that is clearly incorrect; indeed, as atheism is steadily increasing in the civilized world, violence and poverty are steadily decreasing. A person who believes faith is a prerequisite to morality would be unable to explain this relation. Perhaps what is actually meant is that *knowledge* of the existence of God is all that is necessary to acquire morality, but this is also false.

Most animals, including insects, exhibit what appears to be a moral compass. Chimpanzees have been observed to assist other injured chimps climb up trees[4]. As well, certain species of termite display a behavior called suicidal altruism. Upon being invaded by another colony of termites, some members will rupture their own abdomens and explode as a way to block off tunnels from the intruders. The organs and internal fluids are toxic and render the paths inaccessible. *Globitermes sulphureus* is just one species of insect that appears to be willing to die for the survival of their colony[2]. Unless these theists believe that animals are religious, they would be unable to maintain the view that *knowledge* of God is needed for morality. Some religious idealogues, however, could also mean that, whether or not one believes in God or is even aware of the concept, one has a sense of morality because morality is grounded in God.

In order for this view to make sense, it seems there would need to be a sort of medium for God to endow people with morality. What this medium is exactly is unclear. The answer to this problem for some theists would be the soul. This view, however, immediately runs into a multitude of its own problems, specifically those of substance dualism. How exactly can an immaterial substance (the soul) interact with pure material (the body)? A soul exists independent of the body, therefore, if a soul endows people with morality, then the mere physical brain is not at all needed for moral judgments. This implication of Divine Command is completely unsubstantiated by scientific observations so far. Why is it that the moral intuitions of people can be reliably altered by damaging certain parts of the brain? Studies have found that people with ventromedial injuries are twice as likely to admit they would push a fat person in front of a trolly if it meant it would stop the trolly from running over 5 other people. They are also twice as likely to say they would suffocate a baby whose crying would give away them and the position of their family to enemy soldiers[12]. A more egregious example would be the unfortunate case of Charles Whitman.

Whitman was a psychologically stable person before he felt an unexplainable urge to kill his wife and mother as well as random students at the University of Texas. In his suicide note, he confessed he did not know why he wanted to carry out this heinous atrocity and that an autopsy should be performed on his corpse. During the autopsy, a brain tumor was found pressing against his amygdala. This, it is theorized, played a causal role in Whitman's actions[10].

Given that poking around the brain appears to alter a person's sense of right and wrong, it only makes sense to conclude that the brain is the *only* substance responsible for moral judgments. To completely eliminate the idea that a soul is needed to be moral, one need only follow this deduction:

1) The brain is purely physical.
2) A person's sense of morality is mediated by the brain.
3) Therefore, moral judgments are a purely physical phenomenon.

With this view, there does not seem to be any room for God.

In a post-Darwin world, it hardly seems unacceptable to conclude that morality was drummed into the human genome through evolution. An urge to murder your child is clearly not conducive to the survival of the species, so nature selected for those who found infanticide intolerable. The same rule applies for murder, physical aggression of any kind, as well as emotional abuse. Natural selection offers a complete explanation for the origin and grounding of morality.

Sentience and Moral Value

Not every event that can happen has moral value. For example, a gust of wind blowing a few particles of sand in a desert has no moral value. On the other hand, a sober individual walking outside and shooting a child in a stroller does have moral value. The question is then, what exactly is the difference between these two events wherein one has moral value and the other does not? Undoubtedly, the answer is that the presence of sentient beings is required for events to have the quality of being morally good or morally bad.

Imagine a planet in a distant galaxy populated only by rocks. Do moral judgments apply on this planet? Would it be morally bad if a wandering asteroid destroyed a place like this? Most would answer no to these questions. However, if one were to answer yes, there appears to be only four reasons why: 1) it is immoral to break an object into smaller parts, 2) it is immoral to destroy the essence of an object, 3) the planet had the potential to grow life and it is, therefore, morally bad that it was annihilated, or 4) inanimate objects have consciences. All of these reasons have problems. For reason 1, if it were immoral to break an object into smaller parts, then every preschool that allows their students to cut paper for art projects are flagrantly evil; fueling one's car, slicing an apple, sharpening a pencil, and getting a haircut would all be unethical. For reason 2, if it were morally bad to alter the essence of an object, then eating and digesting food would be immoral. For reason 3, if it is immoral to destroy something that has the potential to grow life, then scratching one's nose would be unethical because human skin cells now have the potential to be transformed into viable fetuses with the help of modern technology[6]. If one subscribes to reason 4, then they are reinforcing the idea that the presence of sentience is needed for an event to have moral value and is, thus, self-contradictory.

The idea that moral judgements can apply to a universe completely devoid of animated matter is untenable. Replace the rocks with people on the aforementioned planet and the occurrence of a meteor strike would then have the quality of being good or bad. In order for something to matter, it has to matter *to* someone.

It should be made clear that simply being alive is not enough for something to require moral consideration. Many may oppose this point because it seems obvious that living objects such as plants have moral value; however, here is a *reductio ad absurdum* proof as to why that point of view is untenable:

1) If being alive is all something needs to have moral value, then all living things have moral value.

2) If all living things have moral value, then the bacterium Yersinia Pestis should be treated as a moral agent.
3) Being alive is all something needs to have moral value.
4) Therefore, the bacterium Yersinia Pestis should be treated as a moral agent.

Of course, Yersinia Pestis is the bacterial strain that caused the Black Death and exterminated millions of people in Europe. One who believes being alive is all something needs to deserve moral consideration would have to believe that rickettsiae, malaria, anthrax bacterium, and Clostridium botulinum, a bacterium that produces a neurotoxic chemical that has been used as a biological weapon[5], all deserve to be treated as moral beings. Needless to say, this would be nonsense. If it is nonsense, then being alive is not the only thing an object needs to have moral value; in fact, it is entirely unnecessary. The only thing needed is sentience, or, the capacity to feel emotion.

What Makes an Action Good or Bad?

Now that it is clear that the presence of sentience, or the ability to experience and feel emotion, is required for an action to have moral value, the question then becomes: what exactly makes certain events that affect sentient beings morally good or morally bad?

It has long been held by utilitarian philosophers that actions are bad so long as they cause pain and actions are good so long as they cause happiness. This is known as the Principle of Utility. The idea that maximizing pleasure is morally good has a host of problems attached to it, however. According to this theory, it would be a moral obligation to be constantly high on cocaine until one dies. To circumvent this problem, thinkers such as John Stuart Mill have distinguished between "higher" and "lower" pleasures. Higher pleasures are those associated with wholesome, productive activities such as reading, giving someone a hug, or meditating. Lower pleasures are associated with activities that satisfy primal appetites such as sex, eating, and sleeping[1]. Along with being a simple attempt to save utilitarians from appearing like debauched hedonists, there is much that is unclear about this view. What exactly are the differences between the higher and lower pleasures? Because many of the lower pleasure are required in order to remain alive, how can they be bad at all? And if they are, what is the ideal balance with the higher pleasures? If happiness is the highest virtue, how could it possibly be bad for everyone on Earth to constantly be high on drugs until they all die? The distinction between these pleasures seem to be arbitrary.

Too much can go wrong when one attempts to maximize pleasure. If maximizing pleasure is the only good, then someone who believes torturing and killing people would automatically send the victims to heaven would be morally obligated to do so. ISIS fighters and other Islamic terrorists would be absolved from moral blame under this view because they are all attempting to ascend to heaven; they are simply trying to realize the greatest good. If maximizing pleasure can be dangerous, then it seems logical to conclude that it needs to be completely removed from a well-rounded ethic. The following paragraphs are an explanation and a proof to show that pleasure is not part of the ethical equation at all.

Human well-being exists as a spectrum with three distinct parts. On one end of the continuum exists negative emotion (pain), on the other end exists positive emotion (pleasure), and in between is neutrality. A negative agent is an agent who exists on the left side of the neutral point and is, therefore, experiencing pain. A positive agent is an agent who exists on the right side of the neutral point and is, therefore, experiencing pleasure.

A neutral agent is an agent who falls perfectly on the neutral point and experiences neither pain or pleasure.

The key to understanding why pleasure is not related to ethics is the emotion of *desire*. Desire is a negative emotion; it is negative because it is uncomfortable to want something one does not have. It inspires jealousy and presupposes that one's life is not what they want it to be.

In fact, desire is the *only* thing that places an agent on the negative side of well-being. A negative stimulus doesn't have the quality of being hurtful until one desires it to cease. It is possible for a painful stimulus to not be experienced as painful if one abstains from judging it as being so; a practiced meditator will testify that an agonizing ache in the lower back while sitting can simply be seen as an object of consciousness instead of a painful sensation that requires placation. The following is a *reductio ad absurdum* proof to show that desire is the *only* thing that causes a sensation to be painful. The variable A represents any stimulus normally considered painful (burning one's hand on a stove, for example):

1) If desire doesn't cause A to be painful, then A can be painful without an agent desiring it to stop.
2) If A can be painful without an agent desiring it to stop, then an agent can be indifferent to A and still judge it as painful.
3) Desire doesn't cause A to be painful.
4) Therefore, an agent can be indifferent to A and still judge it as painful.

How can an agent be indifferent to a stimulus and still regard it as painful? Would it not be impossible for the agent to call a stimulus painful if they were truly indifferent to it? The very act of judging precludes the agent from being indifferent. Given the definition of indifference, this argument leads to a contradictory conclusion and is indefensible. Here is a *modus tollens* proof to finalize this idea:

1) If desire doesn't cause painful stimuli to be painful, then an agent can be indifferent to painful stimuli and still judge it as painful.
2) An agent cannot be indifferent to painful stimuli and still judge it as painful.
3) Therefore, desire causes painful stimuli to be painful.

Here is a second proof that demonstrates this same idea:

1) If desire doesn't cause A to be painful, then A can be painful without an agent desiring it to stop.
2) If A can be painful without an agent desiring it to stop, then A can be painful to a being who doesn't feel desire.
3) If A can be painful to a being who doesn't feel desire, then A can be painful to inanimate objects.
4) Desire doesn't cause A to be painful.
5) Therefore, A can be painful to inanimate objects.

Without a doubt, it is absurd to suggest that inanimate objects can feel pain. Here is the *modus tollens* argument that is entailed from this proof:

1) If desire doesn't cause painful stimuli to be painful, then inanimate objects can feel pain.
2) Inanimate objects cannot feel pain.
3) Therefore, desire causes painful stimuli to be painful.

Not only do these proofs show that desire causes stimuli to be painful, they also show exactly how desire is a negative emotion. Negative emotions are painful to experience by necessity; so if desire is the thing that causes a stimulus (either physical, such as breaking a bone, or mental, such as recalling an unhappy memory) to have the quality of being painful, then it must be a negative emotion. In fact, desire is the *one and only* negative emotion. All other emotions that are usually regarded as negative are mere restylizations of desire: anger is the desire to be violent, regret is the desire to go back in time, fear is the desire to protect oneself, depression is the desire to die, etc.

After establishing that desire is the only negative emotion, it becomes clear how pleasure is unrelated to ethics. Because desire is negative, when one feels it, they exist on the negative side of the spectrum of well-being. This means that a being who is completely neutral, not experiencing pain or pleasure, would not feel desire. What's more, a being who exists on the positive end of the spectrum (a positive agent) would not experience desire either. Therefore, they would not desire to *stay* on the positive end of the spectrum; if they did desire to stay on the positive end, then they would immediately shift to the negative end. Thus, decreasing pleasure is not bad and is free of moral value. This is Indifference above the Negative. Here is the first part of the proof that shows how pleasure has no moral value:

1) If desire is a negative emotion, then a positive agent would not experience it.
2) If a positive agent would not experience desire, then a positive agent would not desire to remain positive.
3) If a positive agent would not desire to remain

positive, then decreasing positive emotion is not bad.

4) Desire is a negative emotion.
5) Therefore, decreasing positive emotion is not bad.

Here is the second part of the proof:

1) If increasing positive emotion is morally good, then decreasing it would be morally bad.
2) Decreasing positive emotion is not bad.
3) Therefore, increasing positive emotion is not good.

These two proofs demonstrate that no change in pleasure can have the quality of being good or bad. This means pleasure is devoid of moral value and completely unrelated to ethics. Now the question becomes: if maximizing pleasure is not morally good, then what is?

As stated earlier, the presence of sentient beings are required for actions to have moral value and concomitant with sentience is the ability to feel emotion. Emotions can be categorized into two sections: negative emotion and positive emotion. As previously shown, positive emotion has no moral value. If that is the case, then negative emotion (pain) must be the only thing that has moral value.

Some may say that pain is *sometimes* the grantor of moral value, however that belief has illogical implications; indeed, pain is *always* the grantor of moral value. It is nonsensical to conclude that in one scenario, pain doesn't give an action moral value and in another scenario, it does. That is akin to saying that in some situations, two cubed is equal to eight and in some situations, it isn't. Take, for example, two separate events: Event A and Event B. Event A is morally good and Event B is morally bad. If pain is only sometimes the grantor of moral value, then pain can exist in both scenarios and each one will maintain its designated goodness/badness. Along with pain existing in each scenario, there is a "something else," whatever it may be, that is the true grantor of the specified moral value for these events. If the "something else" is the thing in Event A and Event B that gives each event its respective goodness/badness, then it is the *only* thing that gives each event its respective goodness/badness. Therefore, pain would not be related to the ethics of either of these events. If it is true that pain isn't related to the ethics of this case, then it must be true that pain isn't related to the ethics of every case. This leads to the implausible verdict that pain is not related to ethics at all.

This thought experiment demonstrates that pain and *only* pain has moral value; as shown previously, pleasure is not related to ethics, so if pain is not either, then emotion itself is unrelated to ethics. To show that pain is the *only* thing that has moral value, one need only follow this *reductio ad absurdum* proof:

1) If pain is not related to ethics, then emotion is not related to ethics at all.
2) If emotion is not related to ethics at all, then objects that cannot feel emotion have moral value.
3) If objects that cannot feel emotion have moral value, then inanimate objects have moral value.
4) Pain is not related to ethics.
5) Therefore, inanimate objects have moral value.

As mentioned previously, granting inanimate objects with moral value leads to absurd conclusions; for example, believing inanimate objects have moral value could make it immoral to eat food. This is the concluding proof as to why pain is the *only* thing that has moral value:

1) Either pain is the *only* thing that has moral value or emotion unrelated to ethics completely.
2) Emotion is not unrelated to ethics.
3) Therefore, pain is the *only* thing that has moral value.

As well as demonstrating how pain is the *only* thing with moral value, this proof exposes the absurdity of moral relativism.

How can goodness and badness be purely based on opinion when pain is the *only* thing with moral value? There are only two ways pain can change: it can either decrease or increase. It is easy to tell which of these two is morally good and which one is morally bad. This following proof illustrates how moral relativism is untenable while simultaneously affirming the theory that the reduction of pain is the only good:

1) If pain is the *only* thing with moral value, then decreasing pain is the *only* moral good.
2) Pain is the *only* thing with moral value.
3) Therefore, decreasing pain is the *only* moral good.

With these ideas, it is possible to construct the Universal Ethic. There exists a God-shaped hole in each of our heads and this is what can fill it.

The Universal Ethic

For multiple millennia, ethicists have agonized over the question: what is the all-encompassing rule by which all moral beings should abide? Thinkers have ceaselessly attempted to pinpoint an overarching code that results in perfectly ethical behavior. With the proofs given earlier, the fog surrounding this highly sought-after compass begins to dissipate. This is the Universal Ethic:

> When faced with a choice, the ethical action is *always* the one that decreases the most pain or risk of pain for the most non-immoral agents who are capable of suffering over the longest period of time.

To be clear, an immoral agent is a being who experiences pain from not causing other beings pain. These agents are excluded from the Universal Ethic because attempting to decrease pain for them would result in a paradox. The best thing to do with them, then, is to treat them as devices to decrease pain for the non-immoral agents.

This moral code results in the maximal goodness in the world. It is the ultimate rule that should guide any and all behavior. It explains why it is bad to stab a stranger in the back: because it increases pain. It explains why religious doctrinaires are immoral for committing honor killings for the same reason. It shows why it is bad for a married man to cheat on his wife even if she would never find out: it increases the risk of pain. It shows why it would be immoral to drive while intoxicated even if the driver made it home without causing an accident for the same reason. It illustrates why it would be moral to undergo a painful but necessary surgery: it decreases pain over the longest time. It illustrates why it would be ethical to reprimand a misbehaving child for the same reason.

Non-human animals have moral value as well because they have the capacity to suffer. However, because humans likely experience a deeper and wider array of pain than any other sentient being on Earth, humans are worthy of *more* moral consideration than any other animal. If aliens were to discover mankind and land on Earth and it could be known that they experience richer pain than humanity, then they would be worthy of more moral consideration.

How many, say, dogs have the same value as one human? One answer is that no amount of dogs equal that of one human because each individual dog cannot experience the same amount of pain as a human no matter how many dogs suffer. Another answer is that a limited number of dogs can have the same moral value as a human if the suffering of the dogs is added and is greater than that of the human. The answer here has to be the latter. As previously stated, the only reason why a dog would have less moral value than a human is because they don't experience as deep a sense of pain. Along with non-human animals, other humans can have a shallower sense of pain than other humans. In fact, because the richness of pain likely varies between each and every person, it is guaranteed that there is one person who has the ability to experience deeper pain than any other human on Earth. Therefore, if no amount of dogs equals that of one human, then no amount of humans would equal that of the one person who experiences the richest sensation of pain. This would mean one person has moral dominion over every other sentient being on the planet. This, of course, is absurd. Therefore, a finite number of each non-human animal equals that of one human.

Also included in the Universal Ethic is the agent itself. When considering an action, the agent must keep their own well-being in mind; otherwise, the code would force them to toil themselves to death for the well-being of non-human animals.

Any action that does not decrease pain for beings capable of suffering has no moral value. These actions include behaviors that are widely regarded as unethical in Western culture such as copulating with a dead body or consuming dead relatives. These behaviors are ethically neutral and are only seen as immoral because of cultural biases. In certain South American cultures, not only is it permissible, but it is encouraged to devour deceased relatives[3].

Engaging in activities that actually decrease pain, on the other hand, is a *duty*; deliberately failing to do so renders the agent unethical.

At first glance, following this Universal Ethic appears to encourage attitudes of pro-mortalism and anti-natalism. This, without a doubt, is far from the truth. Pro-mortalism is the idea that not existing is *always* better than being alive. One of the prime objections to negative utilitarianism is what the philosopher R. N. Smart calls the Benevolent World Exploder. If decreasing pain is the ultimate goal of ethics, then it would be a moral duty for a supreme being to instantaneously and painlessly exterminate all of humanity[11]. Though compelling, this argument makes a crucial mistake.

Pro-mortalism is not entailed from the Universal Ethic because death and consciousness cannot exist at the same time. As soon as death occurs, or, specifically, as soon as the brain is rendered entirely inactive, perception and experience cease to exist. Therefore, as a matter of subjective experience, death never happens. It is akin to falling asleep: one only realizes they have fallen asleep after they have woken up. In the Universal Ethic, it states that decreasing pain for beings capable of suffering is morally good. Death cannot decrease pain *for* beings capable of suffering because no being is capable of suffering during/after death. Because no being can experience the bliss of being dead and death does not decrease pain *for* beings capable of suffering, pro-mortalism can *never* be good. Here is a proof to show why pro-mortalism is unjustifiable:

1) Decreasing pain *for* non-immoral agents capable of suffering is the only good.
2) Death does not decrease pain *for* non-immoral agents capable of suffering.
3) Therefore, death is not good.

Anti-natalism, on the other hand, is a different story. Anti-natalism is the idea that it is unethical to have children because, since suffering seems to be integral to the human experience, producing offspring increases the overall pain in the world. However, the theory that having children always increases pain in the universe is patently false. It is possible that a child being born would decrease the overall pain in the world. Albeit birth creates a new being capable of suffering, it is almost always likely that the child will decrease more pain for their parents, siblings, and friends than is created from them being conscious. If it can be known that producing a child will decrease more pain than is created from birthing a new conscience, then having that child would be a moral duty.

The Ethical Calculus

After deducing that decreasing pain or the risk of pain for the most non-immoral agents capable of suffering over the longest period of time is the *only* good, a calculus can be derived that can determine the morality of an action like a math equation. The father of utilitarianism, Jeremy Bentham, formulated the Felicific Calculus centuries ago[7]. His calculus, though creative, greatly lacks scientific substance. In the modern era, creating a scientific and logical calculus is far more doable.

First, it is necessary to quantify pain. This could be done using advanced brain scanning technology because the phenomenon of pain is causally related to physical correlates in the brain[8]. Chemicals such as cortisol, pregnenolone, and thyroid result in the experience of negative emotion. It is possible, though, that a decrease in other chemicals result in negative emotion as well, such as a decrease in estrogen or testosterone. It is likely the proportion of each chemical in the brain is what gives rise to the qualia of pain and, hence, determining this mixture is the key to quantifying it. After developing units of pain using biological correlates, the Ethical Calculus can be derived to measure the morality of any action.

In essence, the calculus determines which of any two competing decisions is most ethical by comparing the total amount of pain that follows each decision. The choice that results in the least amount of suffering is the most ethical. The following hypothetical uses a pregnancy dilemma to illustrate what the formula is and how it can be used.

Say a mother is pregnant and faced with the choice of aborting the child. As soon as the mother makes a choice, whatever it is, two separate universes emerge into existence: the child is born in Universe A and the child is aborted in Universe B. In Universe A, the sum of all negative emotion for all conscious beings is determined for each instance until the death of the last conscious being causally connected to the decision. The sum of negative emotion for each instance is then added together to produce the sum of all negative emotion for all time. This is expressed as $\sum_{S_1=0}^{T} S_1$ where T is the number of instances until the death of the last conscious being causally connected to the decision and S_1 is the sum of all pain for each of those instances. The same method is used for Universe B; the sum of all negative emotion until the end of consciousness in this universe is expressed as $\sum_{S_2=0}^{T} S_2$. To determine which choice is the more ethical of the two, this equation is used: $\sum_{S_1=0}^{T} S_1 - \sum_{S_2=0}^{T} S_2 = M$. If M is a positive number, then the first term is larger and, therefore, having the abortion is the ethical choice. If M is a negative number, then the second term is larger and, therefore, not having the abortion is the ethical choice. This calculus can be used for any dilemma one faces throughout their life.

To reiterate, the Ethical Calculus is as follows:

$$\sum_{S_1=0}^{T} S_1 - \sum_{S_2=0}^{T} S_2 = M.$$

The previous hypothetical uses only two alternative choices, but a decision that has any number of alternative choices can be calculated using the formula. If one is facing a decision that has three alternative choices, for example, then using the calculus is a two step process: 1) randomly select two of the choices and use the equation to determine which one is most moral, then 2) take the championing decision and use the equation to compare it to the third choice. The most moral of any number of choices can be found using this exhaustive approach.

Using this calculus to measure the morality of a choice requires omniscience; however, it demonstrates there is a way to calculate the morality of a decision in theory. Ascertaining the morality of an action is akin to discovering exactly how many atoms are in the universe: it would be nearly impossible to find that answer, but an answer certainly exists.

Diagnosis

The ideas that have been laid out heretofore have certain profound implications. They uncover latent truths about the political circus in modern America and the Absurd.

Every social issue that divides modern America are ethical problems. Abortion, gun control, drug use, euthanasia, and immigration are all moral dilemmas because they relate to a central question: how should human beings be treated to maximize the goodness in the world? The reason why there is so much controversy in regards to social issues is because nearly everyone on either side of every sociological debate appeal to virtue ethics. People who believe there should not be a border wall separating the US and Mexico appeal to virtues such as diversity, freedom, acceptance, and opportunity. People who believe a border wall is a good idea appeal to virtues such as security, safety, order, and civility. The debate then becomes which virtues are more valuable and this, of course, has no answer. Modern politics is essentially two people debating on whether or not chocolate ice cream is better than vanilla. Without the knowledge of what makes certain choices ethical or not, all political discussions reduce to mere personal taste and this is why most social debates are at an impasse.

In reality, every social issue has a correct answer. In regards to these issues, the question that should be asked is this: will this policy reduce the most pain for the most people for the longest time? Whether or not legalizing all drugs would do this has an answer, whether or not building a border wall would do this has an answer, and whether or not banning all automatic guns would do this has an answer. Thus, politics and sociology are fundamentally branches of philosophy and should be treated as such. It is stated in the last section, however, that using the Ethical Calculus requires omniscience and, of course, that will likely never be achieved throughout the course of human history. This leads to the absurdities of morality.

There are two absurdities attached to ethics. The first one is the Self/Other Dichotomy. In order to be an ethical agent, all one has to do is intend on acting in accordance with the Universal Ethic; an agent need not make the right choices to be ethical. Acting in accordance with the Universal Ethic means decreasing pain or the risk of pain for the most non-immoral agents for the longest time *for its own sake*. Without any other motive, one has to abide by this ethic simply because it is the good thing to do. However, quite apocalyptically, this is impossible. One can only abide by the ethic, not because it decreases pain for others, but because it decreases pain for *themselves*.

Because the circuitry has been built into the brain, humans are slaves to their own desires. It has long been postulated by psychologists and philosophers that human beings instinctively seek pleasure and avoid pain. This principle, however, is incorrect. When one examines their psyche closely, they may notice that it is a feeling of distress that causes them to move from one point to another in every instance. One doesn't eat food because it tastes good, rather, one eats food because it's painful being hungry. Even if one eats when they're not hungry, they are still eating to abate pain. This is because they desired to eat and, as previously shown, desire is a painful state of mind. Thus, they still ate to lessen their own pain. This idea that everything humans do are simply attempts to lessen their own pain is true in every scenario: when going to bed, when drinking water, when buying a car, when aimlessly pacing around one's house, etc. The following paragraphs give an explanation and a proof that shows how decreasing pain for oneself controls every voluntary muscle twitch in the body.

It begins with the assertion that wanting something *necessarily* means that the thing in question is not in one's possession. This entails that it is only possible to desire something that one does not have. This further entails that it is not possible to want something one already has. It should be made clear that wanting to *keep* something does not invalidate this idea. When one says they want to keep something, they are essentially saying they want to continue possessing something they already have at a time that is not now. Whether or not one possesses something in the future cannot be known and, therefore, wanting to keep something is equivalent to wanting something one does not know they have.

Another idea related to the proof has been mentioned earlier: desire is a negative emotion. With these two claims, this syllogism that shows it is impossible to desire pain can be constructed:

1) It is only possible to desire what one does not already have.
2) Desire is a negative emotion.
3) Therefore, it is impossible to desire negative emotion (pain).

If one wanted to feel pain, then the feeling of desire would disappear the instant they feel it because they are fulfilling their desire in the act of desiring. To be clear, being unable to desire negative emotion is equivalent to being unable to desire an increase in negative emotion as well.

Along with it being impossible to desire pain, it is also impossible to desire an increase in pleasure. As expressed by Indifference above the Negative, if desire only exists as a negative emotion, then that would entail that desire disappears when one crosses neutrality into the positive end of the spectrum. This would make it impossible to desire any increase in positive emotion. Here is the proof:

1) Positive emotion can only increase if neutrality has already been achieved.
2) Desire disappears at neutrality.
3) Therefore, one cannot desire to increase positive emotion.

The same proof can be used to show that it is impossible to desire a decrease in positive emotion for oneself by simply replacing the word "increase" with "decrease."

If one cannot desire negative emotion, a decrease in positive emotion, or an increase in positive emotion, then there is only one thing left to desire: a decrease in negative emotion. Here is the proof:

1) If desire exists *and* it is impossible to desire an increase in pain, a decrease in pleasure, and an increase in pleasure, then it is only possible to desire a decrease in pain.
2) Desire exists *and* it is impossible to desire an increase in pain, a decrease in pleasure, and an increase in pleasure.
3) Therefore, it is only possible to desire a decrease in pain.

This proof gives one of the premises of the final syllogism. The next premise is related to the value of objects.

It has been noticed by psychologists that humans desire things they value. If one were to get up off their couch to approach their refrigerator, that means they value being in front of their fridge more than sitting on the couch. Conscious beings judge things as being more valuable than others based on personal preference and that is why animals move their bodies. The syllogism that shows that humans only move to acquire things they desire goes as follows:

1) One can only move their body to acquire valuable objects or experiences.
2) Valuable objects and experiences are desirable.
3) Therefore, one can only move their body to acquire things that are desirable.

Now, after proving the two premises, the proof that demonstrates how the pursuit of lowering pain for oneself is the sole motivation that moves the human body goes as follows:

1) One can only move their body to acquire things that are desired.
2) It is only possible to desire a decrease in pain for oneself.
3) Therefore, one can only move their body to decrease pain for oneself.

This fact gives rise to the Self/Other Dichotomy.

The *only* way to be ethical is to sincerely wish to decrease pain for the most agents for the longest time. The *only* thing that drives human behavior is decreasing pain for oneself and oneself only. This divorce between what is good and what is actually enacted means everyone is destined to be immoral. Even if one wanted to devote every calorie of their being to realizing the Universal Ethic, they would do so only because it would pacify a negative feeling of desire, guilt, or inferiority to take up such a cause. *Everything* one does is innately selfish; the kindest acts one can think of are done in the name of egoism. One only donates to charity because *they* want to, one only decides to volunteer at a homeless shelter because *they* want to, and one only decides to have a child because *they* want to. Decreasing pain for oneself is a prison that none can escape. It is impossible to be moral; no one is a saint.

Perhaps, because an ethic that should be adhered to should also be one that is possible to adhere to (ought implies can), what makes an agent ethical isn't intending on decreasing pain for its own sake but, instead, the pairing of the Universal Ethic with their desires. With this view, to be an ethical agent, one need only will themselves so that embodying the Universal Ethic decreases the pain they experience. This can be done by persuasion and instilling a belief in one's self that acting in such a way is the greatest possible good.

Though this isn't explicitly related to ethics, it is interesting to note that these proofs illuminate why the human experience seems to be marked by a pervasive feeling of sadness and dissatisfaction. If we can only move our bodies to lessen pain for ourselves, then what does that say about our day to day lives? Since people are constantly moving from the moment they awake to the moment they fall asleep, it stands to reason that every waking moment is accompanied by some amount of misery. Even the most minute movements are motivated by pain: moving one's eyes, shifting one's feet, raising one's eyebrows, speaking, as well as thinking itself. We only move when our minds are disturbed; contentedness lies within the blank spaces between each action, each word, and each thought. For every downtrodden soul, the best advice is to stop moving; happiness is only released when it ceases its escape.

The second absurdity related to morality is the Absurdity of Decision Making. Because calculating the goodness of actions require precognition, one can only know they have made the right choice after they have already made it, and perhaps not even then. Some choices have likelier answers than others. Dilemmas such as whether or not one should crash their car into the vehicle in front of them has a safe choice. However, in reality, it is possible that crashing one's car into the person in front of them could decrease more pain in the world than not: perhaps the person in the other car, having spent all their money on repairs, decides to buy a lottery ticket and, with incredible luck, wins millions. The car crash would then be seen as a true deliverance, so even this choice does not have a clear answer. The absurdity becomes even more obvious when considering puzzles such as who one should marry, when to have a child, or what one should do for a living. Asking oneself what the answers are to these questions is a useless endeavour. The rightness or wrongness of an action can never be known with only the mere human mind.

It is commonly believed that, when faced with a choice, the agent will regret one choice and be proud of the other. This is simply not the case. As Søren Kierkegaard has made clear, it is possible to regret all decisions[9]. When choosing whether or not to marry, it is plausible that one will regret both decisions if one could reverse time to make both choices. Not only that, but regret is not constant. It is possible to regret making a choice immediately after doing it and then deciding it was the right choice after some time has passed. Give it a little more time and it is possible to regret the decision once more. Not only can it not be known if any choice is ethical, it cannot even be known how an agent will view their own decisions.

This disconnect between wanting to make the right choices and the essence of consequence is the Absurdity of Decision Making. We all want to be certain that we make the right decisions, yet it cannot be known if the choices we make are correct; this truth manifests itself in the psyche as anxiety.

We imagine that there exists a perfect form of us that makes the right choice in every situation. This form plays the game perfectly; it makes every correct choice from the moment of birth until the moment of death. We try our hardest to embody this form but it is not possible to know if one is. In reality, it is exorbitantly likely that one steers far from the perfect form as quickly as it can happen. The best thing to do then is to try and be the perfect form after each subsequent decision. In a universe that hides everything behind closed doors, one can only accept they almost certainly have the wrong key.

Though somewhat bleak, this ethical code sheds light on how one should deal with loss. A loss is simply any wrong decision. They are losses because they incur non-optimal consequences in the universe and thus, preclude one from experiencing the greatest good they could have if they made the right decision. People often think of terminating a life-long friendship, not getting accepted into a desired university, or missing out on a chance to ask someone on a date as losses. However, give it enough time, and it is possible that events like these actually have better consequences than not. For example, breaking up with someone who was once thought of as the love of one's life could be beneficial if both partners find people who are better for each of them in the future. Someone who discovers a fruitful career playing a musical instrument would look back on their failure to enter medical school as a fortunate event.

Without knowing your future causal chain, it is always possible that a loss can be a gain.

Sources

1. Bhardwaj, Kiran. "Higher and Lower Pleasures and our Moral Psychology." *Res Cogitans*, 2010, commons.pacificu.edu/cgi/viewcontent.cgi?article=1003&context=rescogitans.
2. Bordereau, C., et al. "Suicidal defensive behaviour by frontal gland dehiscence in Globitermes sulphureus Haviland soldiers (Isoptera)." *Insectes Sociaux,* 1997, link.springer.com/article/10.1007/s000400050049.
3. Cowie, Ashley. "Bizarre, Brutal, Macabre And Downright Weird Ancient Death Rituals." *Ancient Origins*, ancient-origins.net/history-ancient-traditions/ancient-death-rituals-0010973.
4. De Boer, J. "Moral ape philosophy." *Biology & philosophy*, 2011, ncbi.nlm.nih.gov/pmc/articles/PMC3215880/.
5. Dhaked, Ram Kumar, et al. "Botulinum toxin: bioweapon & magic drug." *The Indian journal of medical research*, 2010, ncbi.nlm.nih.gov/pmc/articles/PMC3028942/.
6. "Embryo stem cells created from skin cells." *ScienceDaily*, 2019, sciencedaily.com/releases/2019/05/190502143437.htm.

7. "Hedonic Calculus." *Utilitarianism*, utilitarianism.com/felicalc.htm.
8. Phillips, M. L., et al. "Neurobiology of emotion perception I: The neural basis of normal emotion perception." *Biological psychiatry*, 2003, ncbi.nlm.nih.gov/pubmed/12946879.
9. Popova, Maria. "Either/Or: Kierkegaard on the Tyranny of Choice and How to Transcend the Trap of Double Regret." *Brain Pickings*, brainpickings.org/2016/05/05/either-or-kierkegaard/.
10. "Report to the Governor, Medical Aspects, Charles J. Whitman Catastrophe." *CI Media*, 1966, alt.cimedia.com/statesman/specialreports/whitman/findings.pdf.
11. Smart, R. N. "Negative Utilitarianism." *Utilitarianism*, utilitarianism.com/rnsmart-negutil.html.
12. Young, L., et al. "Damage to ventromedial prefrontal cortex impairs judgment of harmful intent." *Neuron*, 2010, sciencedirect.com/science/article/pii/S0896627310001728.

Printed in Dunstable, United Kingdom

64859417R00031